BACK RIVER

VERSE BY
JIM GRONVOLD

BACK RIVER

VERSE BY
JIM GRONVOLD

Oak Ink Press
2017

Copyright © 2013 James Gronvold
All rights reserved
Revised edition 2017

ISBN-10: 0-9987189-3-9
ISBN-13: 978-0-9987189-3-4

Typesetting: Wordsworth, San Geronimo, CA
Cover photo: Ann Gronvold

To order additional copies of Back River
or to contact the author, write:

Oak Ink Press
oakinkpress@icloud.com

To Ann

Contents

Back River	1
Brown Pelicans	2
Big Sur	4
Pfeiffer Beach	5
Dune Grass	6
Eared Grebes	7
Chimney Swifts	8
European Robin	9
Black-Headed Gull	10
Mallard	11
Redwings	12
Merlin	13
Buckeye Hill	14
Hills	15
Trail	16
Pebbles	17
Brook	18
Pond	19
Boston Harbor	20
Sailing Home	21

Copenhagen	22
Ven	24
Altitude	26
Fog	27
Nonfiction	28
Oak	29
Back Porch	30
300 Canada Geese	31
Returning	32
Sparrows	33
Drifts	34
Tidal Ice	35
Ice Candles	36
Milky Way	37
Wealth	38
Bipeds	39
Wonder	40
Pictures	41
Answers	42
Quest	43

Back River

On a seesaw river
between houses
and harbor.
Between proud hill
and humble sand

the leaping ocean
crawls past forest
into salt marsh
and spawning streams

weaving strands
of sea and land
bursting at their
watery seams.

On this fertile mud
grasses spire
and here we touch
the sacred place
where we crawled
off our bellies
with reptilian grace
and rose from
the hallowed mire.

Jim Gronvold

Brown Pelicans

A silent procession
of pelicans
glides single file
past breaking surf

coasting a breath
above curling water
that crashes
a wingtip away.

Holding their
tight formation
they skate over
rolling waves.

Then spotting
a shoal of shiny prey

flap to a stop
twist and dive

hit the ocean
like daggers

Back River

stab the brine
and grab what they can

then calmly rise
and are on their way

riding the sliding
shore to the bay.

Big Sur

Brilliant coast.
Beatific mist.
Eternity in a view.

Deep shades of sea reflect
heaven's earthly hue.

Streams pray to their ocean
meadows rise into blue.

Hillsides ride the sea breeze
that drifting clouds pursue

and cliffs drop down to coves
from a highway winding through.

Pfeiffer Beach

Under the huge hand of sky
at the fingertips of wind

the power behind this ocean—
curling its sandy toes—

grinds the crumbling coast
with wild indifference

the way the heavens spin
in cosmic innocence.

Dune Grass

Sparse grasses
on high dunes
spun by turning sky

carve Zen circles
on crawling sand

into windmill
grinding wheels

that scatter
their hopeful rye

over the beach
drifting from land

and the sea
returning to sky.

Eared Grebes

Ocean corks
bobbing off shore
vanish when I blink.

Diving from surface
they tuck their wings
kick into jackknives
uncoiling like springs

pierce the ocean
and disappear

only to pop up
anywhere
bouncing about
on the sparkly glare.

Jim Gronvold

Chimney Swifts

Chimney Swifts chitter
in ticking down sun

climb, twist and roll
with gliding ease

chasing tiny prey
over heaven's shore.

Spirits of seal
on reflections of sea

squeeze perfect turns
in the blink of a breeze

until the sun
sinks out of sight

and they dive back down
abandoned chimneys

like ghosts of smoke
rewound into cinder

to sleep in ashes
and awaken in flight.

European Robin

A barrel-chested
little balladeer

roaming gardens
and countryside

announces himself
loud and clear

in a voice ringing
with fierce pride.

Blushing from
crown to chest

he brushes all
caution aside

and wearing his
heart on his vest

his love is a joy
he cannot hide.

Jim Gronvold

Black-Headed Gull

Sliding over
slate rooftops

a bright gull sails
the dull gray—

a slice of sun
cracks the cloud—

he turns on a tip
of sharpened feather

shoots down a shaft
of moving light

tilts between spires
shouts past chimneys

and drops like a bolt
from thunderous height

onto a crowd
of his flocking brothers

scattering them
into squawking flight.

Mallard

A clatter of mallard
on the winding flow
dunking, flapping,
wagging in circles

their ripples lapping
over each other
as they paddle
into an easy row
and chatter off
around the bend

slapping the banks
with buoyant echoes
as the river
swallows their shadows.

Redwings

A screaming
of redwings
over the river

shouting and
beating the air

above a shape
on the water
that I couldn't
make out
in the sun's
blinding glare.

Then I saw
the cross of
dark feathers
floating face down
on the tide

and the birds began
to murmur
as the last ripples died

and I heard
their sad confusion
drift over the riverside.

Merlin

A merlin sniper
in high branches
tracking the air traffic
flapping below

calculates speed
and range in a blink

her whole body
a tightly strung bow

she pulls herself
into a point
and shoots down an arc
just over her prey
to deliver a single blow.

Buckeye Hill

Footpaths wander
rolling meadows
of grazing cattle
and whispers of cloud.

Lark Sparrows
light on their toes
sing like laughter
dreaming out loud.

And downwind of
buckeyes in bloom
the sweet tangled air
is slippery with swallows.

Hills

Shaded valleys
crease golden tan hills

that stretch to the coast
and the soft warm sand

where they cool their heels
in the curling spills

at the ocean edge
of this graceful land.
.

Trail

Through lichen lace
and mossy shade
the trail winds
in and out of shadow.

It rises and falls
against the hills

cuts along
a rocky hollow

slithers down
a slippery grade

to sun itself
on warm rock

before weaving back
through the meadow.

Pebbles

Pebble spangled
gleaming stream.

Polished rainbows
set in stone.

Every rock
a precious gem

even after
the spring flows

when they turn back
to gravel and sand.

Brook

From the footbridge
what looked like
a butterfly shadow
on quivering stone
in the brook below

turned out to be
a water strider
skimming the
shimmering sheen

dining on
shiny morsels
caught in her
radiant halo.

Pond

Light speck insects
over the pond
excite a waxwing ballet.

Barnstorm swallows
mow down mosquitos
in an open air buffet

as a blue heron statue
lifts floating feathers
and slowly climbs away.

Boston Harbor

Driving over the old bridge
surrounded by morning sky

water color reflections
caught me as I slid by.

Nets of rolling prisms
crisscrossing the bay.

Stained glass panes
on floating webs

woven by workboats
plowing their rows

through the wakes
of broken rainbows

and my heart
as I drove away.

Sailing Home

Hiked out on a port tack
toward a sunset splashing
gold on blue water.

Balanced on a breeze
and the beating spray
you might catch a glimpse
of sinking treasure
in the sliding seconds of last light

and smell the salt aroma of home
as the shore drifts into night.

Jim Gronvold

Copenhagen

On a bench in the sun
and antique shade,
by a quiet canal
I fold my paper.

A few sleeping boats
wake to one passing
and calmly scratch
their backs on old tires.

Orange tiled roofs
frame October skies
as I bounce over cobbles
on pedals and spokes

fenders rattling down
stone rippled streets.

I crease blue puddles
with easy strokes

turn into currents
of boulevard

Back River

cruise to the gate
of a king's garden

and coast down a path
to a ring of benches
around a fountain
in a circle of trees

I shake out the pages
of yesterday's news—

a ripple of leaves
rolls under me—

and I lean back
on a gentle breeze.

Ven

For about a year
the gull would appear
on the tiled rooftop
behind the kitchen.

I'd raise my arm
to toss a scrap

he'd swoop
into a smooth glide
and scoop it
out of the air—
every morning
in any weather—

then suddenly
he wasn't there.

Months passed
it was time to leave.

Back River

Then
on my last day
in Copenhagen
I heard my friend's
familiar cry.

I raised my arm
and he threw me
a gliding wave
of last goodbye.

Jim Gronvold

Altitude

The wide Pacific
falling below

in slow rows
of woven ocean

rolling under
my window.

At forty thousand
they barely move,

but threading waves
are weaving lace

all the way
to San Francisco.

Fog

From the high road
the whole valley
had turned into cloud.

I drove down
through deep fog
and the sun shrank
to an eerie glow.

Then up from where
the shore would be
if there were more
than mist to see

a cedar dragon shadow
rose on the steam
of the phantom lake
and the wispy breath
of a mystic tree,

like a ghost
of ancient fantasy
raising its head
in front of me.

Jim Gronvold

Nonfiction

Leaves type
scribbling rain.

Waves recite
rhyming seas.

Planets scribe
sacred spirals

and stars rewrite
their galaxies.

Oak

In the shade of a shedding oak
a whisper of bone dry brushes.

Each note the stroke of a fallen leaf
touching down with a tap.

Unheard on their own
but with so many others
their voices overlap

rustling into a drumroll—
a requiem for summer.

Jim Gronvold

Back Porch

Autumn morning
blue marble sky.

Tea on the porch.
River drifting by.

Leaves land on water
and glide to the bay.

A leaf lands on me
and I wish I could stay.

300 Canada Geese

Hundreds of honkers
keeping pace
in a line too long
for their usual V

on winds too strong
for wasted breath
or casual
cacophony.

A rolling line
of unwinding knots
slipping out of view.

Breaking links
beating their way
back into a chain

of flapping commas
dashing to dots
that disappear
in distant rain.

Jim Gronvold

Returning

Over and over
since the sun knows when
clouds reappear and unroll.

Winds turn curling pages
lifted from scrolling waves

rewriting the open skies
with the breath of brine and dew.

Clouds disappear before our eyes
but will always rise anew

as ancestors returning
crawling out of the blue.

Sparrows

Out of the snow bright sky
sparrows are dropping like stones.

Slamming their brakes
into slow motion

just in time to grab a twig
in the spear tipped tangle

of leafless bones
that dance the stabbing wind.

Jim Gronvold

Drifts

Arctic air
sweeping low
over slow waves
of drifting snow
blowing over
huddled sparrows.

A stinging stream
of diamond wind
swirls around
the hollow shadows
behind those
hunkering heroes
outside my
kitchen window.

Tidal Ice

Ice floes crowd
the sinking river.

Frozen sheets
of fallen sky.

Frosted shards
of shattered mirror.

Scattered puzzle
pieces of cloud

melting back
to the ocean

while ascending
on a sigh.

Jim Gronvold

Ice Candles

On rare nights
when the salt marsh
is covered in blue snow

when the air is clear
and the tide is low

a shining moon
may sparkle
through clusters
of broken ice

and magical lights
might appear

like flickering
candled windows

along the shivering river
where silver moonlight flows.

Milky Way

Star sand
in a cosmic ocean

drifting through
the endless wide

on ripples and waves
that somehow expand
into the ever unknown

in ways I need not understand
to make its wonder my own.

Wealth

Moments of wonder
are the real treasure,
the gold no one can steal.

The opening of leaves.
The rising of the sun.

The way that everything
is part of everyone.

Bipeds

We are the ember dust of stars
that crawled our way to standing

shimmering specks electric
reflecting each other's spark.

We are our ancestor's echoes
stumbling out of the dark

learning to walk with every step
as we stride the wide expanding.

Jim Gronvold

Wonder

From the beat of a single pulse
back to the cosmic beginning

powers of cause and effect
set the galaxies spinning

in ways that rhyme our waves
and chime our skies to thunder

in ways that open orchids
and move our hearts with wonder.

Pictures

Take a still picture
of a rushing stream.

Film a waterfall
or a breaking wave.

Splash digital drops
in microchip caves

to trap the sight
of flowing light

turning inside out,
falling through frames,

to hold what cannot be held—
flickering water-flames.

Answers

Enter the light
of a bright leaf

a flaming cloud
or a spark of sand.

Feel the might
of a distant sun

a wild river
or a meadowland.

Follow the scent
of answers

as questions
arise and expand.

And delight in
the mortal moment

of trying
to understand.

Quest

On the way
to everywhere
we may stop
at many wells
some are tainted

some are true
some just shimmer
on thin air

but the river
that we carry
in every cell we bear
is deep and full of stars
already everywhere.

www.ingramcontent.com/pod-product-compliance
Lightning Source LLC
Chambersburg PA
CBHW070553300426
44113CB00011B/1888